flor ~ a ~ muse

B. Monét & Z. Rose

BALBOA.PRESS
A DIVISION OF HAY HOUSE

Balboa Press books may be ordered through booksellers or by contacting:

Balboa Press
A Division of Hay House
1663 Liberty Drive
Bloomington, IN 47403
www.balboapress.com
844-682-1282

Because of the dynamic nature of the Internet, any web addresses or links contained in this book may have changed since publication and may no longer be valid. The views expressed in this work are solely those of the author and do not necessarily reflect the views of the publisher, and the publisher hereby disclaims any responsibility for them.

The author of this book does not dispense medical advice or prescribe the use of any technique as a form of treatment for physical, emotional, or medical problems without the advice of a physician, either directly or indirectly. The intent of the author is only to offer information of a general nature to help you in your quest for emotional and spiritual well-being. In the event you use any of the information in this book for yourself, which is your constitutional right, the author and the publisher assume no responsibility for your actions.

Any people depicted in stock imagery provided by Getty Images are models, and such images are being used for illustrative purposes only.
Certain stock imagery © Getty Images.

Print information available on the last page.

ISBN: 978-1-9822-5318-9 (sc)
ISBN: 978-1-9822-5319-6 (e)

Balboa Press rev. date: 02/18/2022

Contents

According to Webster Dictionary:

flora - **flora** (n) / flohr-*uh*/
    1. all the plants growing in a certain region or period, listed by species and considered as a whole.
    2. an enumeration of them, generally with a guide to their identification (e.g. the present volume, the Flora of Victoria, the Flora of New South Wales and so on). In this case 'flora' is written with a capital F

flowers fall on the floor,
but before that
they grew more wise.

dream bigger
love stronger
live better
rise farther

home is the land
home to the Lady

Powerful
Beautiful
Soundful
Joyful
are you led to the land
home to Lady Flora

- B. Monét & Z. Rose

dedicated to:
friends and family

It wouldn't be so amusing if all we shared were confusing young-adult flower poems. Nature isn't everyone's style, but it happens to be the reason we get along and want to collaborate. We love each other's perspectives and hope you find these poems to be the support to evolve. Growing is hard, not all the plants make it. This is a fact of life. This book shares the uncommon opinion, and we do not uproot an opinion because it is not common. We write the realities of these flowers and their experiences we see planted for them. With these restrictions in our personal lives, it brought change to the perspective and the words we chose. These carefully picked out poems express our stories in letter form and our artistic notes in poetic form. We are women of: many forms, many faces, many opinions.

We write blogs, books, and bumper stickers. We are down to earth friends[1] that want to share their love for flowers and poetry. Please feel free to reach out to us to collaborate, follow, and interact. Please know we all do our best to be there for each other, but if there is something urgent, reach out to a professional. As we would love to say we are experts, we are always learning and growing. This is part of the process. We relate a lot of what we do to the world around us. Like letting the wind be a guide in the direction our leaves blow. We bloom in the Spring and plant seeds inside for the winter. The seasons help encourage change and growth each year. Sometimes we are transplanted, sometimes there are other circumstances that change; yet nature runs her course. Nature surrounds us, influences us, and moves us.

We are so moved by what nature is calling out about and want to make a difference. We help people see nature and their very nature in a different perspective. Artist and creative minds are supporters of change and growth. Nature holds these flower children near her heart. We don't speak for the flowers, nor anyone else. We find inspiration with nature, and other brilliant minds. One brilliant photographer and poet, Dan Slee, inspired

---

[1] Footnote about friends:
B. Monét and Z. Rose met in college. A lot happened, but what changed was their spiritual connection to the world. Written in their blog, seen in their art.

us to continue writing. The perspective it takes to stop and smell the roses hidden off the path takes courage—a muse that pays off. Being one with earth enhances energy, encourages excitement, and gives purpose. Take in each page like it is a fragrance of a flor-a sharing a-muse.

welcome
to a new beginning

                    Wake up:

opening slowly,
but carefully

                 warmed slowly,
                    and gently

                                    stretching slowly,
                                         yet tenderly

                 moved emotionally,
                    but suddenly

living passionately,
yet purposefully

                    - Z. Rose

                         1

i count down time
like petals off a fresh flower.
will he be the one
or will she.
time knows no wrong
only fixing who has been wronged.
growing from gravel
yearn for love, in a drought.
i countdown my minutes
never forgetting to take my time.

    - Z. Rose

Dear Beauty,

Don't look away,
i'm unpredictable.
growing taller to see everything
feeling the Sun's rays grin my way

blooming for power
crawling with ambition
her rosy cheeks are pinched,
and she vanished through my fingers.

-an admirer

- Z. Rose

like the weather changes
i'm changing
like the leaves falling
i'm changing
like the petals weakening
i'm changing
like the breeze freezing
i'm changing

i've changed
light to frost
i've changed
now lights out
i've changed
don't take it personally

- B. Monét

4

sun kissed and free, i smile
caressed and amused, i giggle
hidden and unseen, i worry

she won't make it

past winter, i wilt
breaking apart, i dormant
i've lost it, yet i'm rooted

− B. Monét

you see those specs of yellow
out on the field
those wildflowers who dance freely
as the wind rushes by
as the storm passes by
i wish i were like them

timid, shut from reality
the morning tussles
the sun is rising
bold, i bloom free

- B. Monét

delicate like a sunflower,
i rise when the sun is out
t a l l, i stand, proud as can be
time rushes by, as the sun fades away

memories are made
sun kissed, i'm pleased
memories are eased
i bow, watching the last glimpse of light
f
     a
        l
           l
             when i don't feel it's warmth

-B. Monét

Today I woke up.
The sun came through the leaves of a large tree. Reaching
up to the clouds, stretching my patience and testing my
balance I found peace in my yoga practice. The beautiful
scenery was a-muse for me to push myself harder. Standing
in a tree-pose I found myself wanting to go on an
adventure. Though it is comfortable to stay grounded, I
found myself without perspective. Transplanting myself
outside, I found myself listening to the stories the
wind told and the blown perspective out of the clouds.
It wasn't always the truth, but somehow it was a little
right. I found the rocks near my roots are not to keep
me from growing, but raise me like the sun rises.

Dear Auntie,

the wind whistles through my petals
one blowing off in the night.
oh no, now i'll never get picked,
to bring joy and love to all that pass by.
So i stand tall not to poke a soul.

will you take me in?

i'll teach the baby sprouts:
how to stand and root deep
how to sing and attract the bees
how to bleed and water when in need
how to grow and prune a sweet tune

i love your magnificent colors
i could work on my sun tan, too
it seems i can't keep my color after a season,
or two.

oh, how i dream to be picked, too.
first flower to shine brighter, than a diamond
second best sun soaker, so chic
third best lover, what a story

i will do anything to be seen or heard
each time the wind whistles, i dance

yet one day a storm will take me away.
i hope you'll take me in,
hopefully we'll see each other again.

- favorite niece*

*(aka: twice transplanted, newly started)

- Z. Rose

a spine stands tall and holds a mind,
two cockscombs stand side by side.
similar, yet different

the mind begins to travel in time:

regret is pondered on, from the past
worries are ignored, in the present
and fear is overwhelmed, by the future

emotions run, trying to understand:
do opposites attract?
or are we so similar,
we retract?

- B. Monét

slicing my bloom, in two
splitting my stem, in half
shards of bark cover my roots
stabbing myself in the back

sabotaging gossip wipes my color
sunburns expose my rusting leaves
suffering to survive like a vine
stealing nutrients in search for more life

stabbed, into groundwater
simpler times were cultivated
scared, it's too late
secrets buried me alive

- Z. Rose

dipping the tip in
drowning in dirty water
picking up the top
letting the roots rot
sorrows heard past the sunset
nowhere to run
the tip split through
the tip in two

- Z. Rose

take time to smell the roses—
even if you can't find them

- Z. Rose

Garden Handled:

i feel like a fraud
your eyes chain me to be perfect
competition sets a fire in me

the need to be
brighter
stand taller
stand longer
under direct stare

i am safe as i grow, sound
picked and ready
i'd say i wasn't
but the gardener knows best

   - Z. Rose

Gardenias:

we work so hard
sweating blood to water our flowers
we work so hard
tilling the land with our nails
we work so hard
singing praise in His name to guide life
we work so hard
buckling our knees to the ground
we work so hard
fetching buckets of water not to drink
we work so hard
providing a home to rest in
we work so hard
feeding those sweet enough to visit

we work so hard,
yet beauty isn't enough;
nor building a home,
nor creating life

we work so hard
to have it all destroyed

- Z. Rose

Singing in the Sun:

the light warms my lips
opening my mouth to speak
i feel a tug on my colorful style
tongue tied up in a kiss

i open my eyes to realize where i am

trapped in a moment until i blush
trapped in the memories of a child
laying down the royal flush
i dance away into the wild

picking up my roots
a beat in my heart motivates me close
a tune makes me turn in your arms
sing to me when the sun goes down

i know you'll break life's curse

- Z. Rose

Firecracker:

simple with beauty from within

yelling for attention
watching her grow, past my line of sight

moving on, over my head
she sees, past my back
overpowering, with beauty
not stopping, shattering the mirror

unable to see what she's become
a dimorphic bloom

beauty, simply from within

— Z. Rose

```
        delicate like a rose
         fetal, as an infant
       bleeding like a red rose
         crying, as an infant
      growing thorns like a rose
        babbling off, as an infant
        petals fall like a rose
      sleeping more, as an infant

              - Z. Rose
```

as she heats
her petals open

as he enters
his thorns draw blood

- Unwanted Beauty

- Z. Rose

Dear Beauty,

I'm sorry it was hard to see you there. If I hadn't squinted I wouldn't have seen the way you secretly stayed hidden. In the haze, forgotten. As if to be beautiful meant to be invisible. Those that have fame are swarmed to be known— sell the secrets. Yet beauty is unique like each individual. Many pass, but I had stopped before a-muse. An inspiration to be spread. I'll let the others know you are here, within.

~ Wildfire

A Rose:

falling into a rose bush
body stabbed by thorns
awoken by bright spears
glass shattering through my throat
choking on blood

drowning

bubbles trail to the surface
in the purple haze, i'm faint
drawn to the surface
confused by the foreign touch
fighting to release myself

failure perches on my shoulder
repeating every mistake
scolding the soul until she has third degree burns

home of disease and death
i've given up, why don't you

blind with rose-dirt paint in his eyes
tears wash my color into rivers
revealing the key i trusted only you with

hypnotized by your heroic beauty
i throw all my brushes in a river

distracted dancing downtown
love painted me a dress
yet you see through me

inspired, to paint a rose
betrayal and love resembled

- Z. Rose

Forget Me Not:

a flower
bursting open for attention
picked and ooed

smells of joy
curiosity
happiness
begins to wilt A

W

A

Y

i said, forget me not
but now, it is gone
has beauty been forgotten?
or have i?

- Z. Rose

when you were fake to me
saying it was an early Spring
feeling warm to the touch
running fingers through my hair
chasing wind for a kiss

but you turned on me
back to your old ways
shutting down
shutting out the town
i knew the whole time

i didn't want to believe it

it was always you
every year, coming and going
lying and defying
what i know to be true
well this Spring i lied

it's my turn to come early

but i died
you froze my heart cold
now i lay fake
no emotion
no life

crumpling at every touch
color fading like the days
casually tortured with memories
caught up in feeding the lies
pretending it is still Spring

- Z. Rose

light pink petal powder
snuffed straight,
to make my mind straight
hustling around my garden.

cultivating flame flowers
burning at the touch
burning through the books
burning through the eyes
burning through the word of mouth
growing better than imagined

am i to congratulate?
am i to blame?
was that me?
how was she remembered?

her flowers had an impact,
i believe that was me.

   - Z. Rose

Love Like a Lilac:

Love is like a Lilac
there sometimes,
other times on her own
loyal, but independent
possessive to everyone
everything is hers

step aside
find a step
the beat hits
the coin flips
hers, but she'll share
time is spent for a price

if anything is forever, i hope love is

like a Lilac,
planted for life
blooming sometimes,
other times failing
starting again, gaining energy
cultivating love

unknowingly deserving
of her parents
love of others
dreams and more
struggling to stand,
Lilacs still Love

- Z. Rose

you hold a secret tucked in the shell of your seed

tell me your story
breaking the silence with a laugh
tell me your story
avoiding questions, jokingly dismissing me
tell me your story
slacking to cover your tracks
tell me your story
an artificial flower, more like a weed

you have deception written all over your eyes

- B Monét

Chrysanthemum's Pain:

hardly open, i hesitate to show my light—
the one i hide deep inside my shell

i would shine so bright that
the sun would bathe me in kisses

those who travel from afar will stop,
and watch me glisten

suddenly i wilt, dramatically i fall
i'm torn.

never fully grown
now i'm hardly o p e n

- B. Monét

Chrysanthemum's Aura:

i'll read to you as you sleep,
make sure no one steals your glow
protectively rationing water—
overflowing with rage
there's so much i've done,
but nothing can be done

my flower has been labeled as a weed

She's not overgrown—
it's called confidence.
She's not taking opportunities—
it's called equality.
She's not a burden—
it's called inner peace.

corrupt from the outside in
she rests to share her aura

-    Z. Rose

Lily's Freedom:

sound the bells—
dust off the Fine China,
that sits on the top of the shelves

water the vines, dangling from the walls
set up the table to entertain
those who visit from afar

roll out the long
Gold
Carpet

let the
town
city
state
nation
know
that i have
b l o o m e d

    - B. Monét

Petunia's Resentment:

i have this feeling—
constantly looking over my shoulder
a stem split evenly in half—
as if someone is breathing down my neck

chills run down my spine
anticipating whether an insult will puncture my spirit

watch as my blood runs deep—
will it sour my expression
watch as a wet match sparks—
allow rage to pour out my mouth

- B. Monét

Did the Daisy:

Did the Daisy dream about you
Did you wish you never knew
Did the Daisy draw in your notebook
Did you burn it with all your memories
Did the Daisy dress up, and take you out
Did you stand up, and say no
Did the Daisy dare you to jump
Did you take the leap of faith

    - Z. Rose

Today I'm feeling like a flor-a.
I see beauty in the little buds coming onto the tree.
I sweep over the brush and see a dazzling daisy.
Did you see that? Did they want to play? A patch of
daisy's dream over a wave and surprise me with a
smile on my face. I'm not invisible. I'm not fake. I
believe in myself to grow today. Up to town we go!

Bells that Sing:

the bells ring
for the wedding down the hill
for the graduation party down the street
for the baby shower downstairs
for the alarm waking you from a dream

the bell rings
for Spring
for Stamen
for Love
for You

   - Z. Rose

Follow My Cardinal Rules:

1.Never open your petals before noon

2.Drink up all the sun for fun

3.Attract the men, but want the bees

4.Symbolize elegance, but take power

5.Fight for what is right

6.Be ready to turn a new leaf

- Z. Rose

Dear daily blooms,

We want to make sure the time we are closed off does not take from Spring's growth. We want to make sure we follow these rules to ensure purity, for beauty and simple incentives. There is enough temptations driving over the new starts. We must preserve what we have, to embrace the power we have; symbolizing elegance. The power is within the world around; the sun, bees, and moon provide a-muse. Stay planted for what is right and I will keep you safe.

~ Mother Nature

Eyes on the Globe:

trapped looking at the same twig
watching it decompose at my feet
dreading the day my hair starts to fall too
not taking the time to enjoy my youth
my beauty only lasts a season
Picked, Plucked, and Pruned
stuck here on this globe
Wondering, Wishing, Wanting
adventure to walk up to me
take me from this globe
and show me a new world
to prove to myself there is more
more to the cycle of life
trapped at eye level with the twig
seems the world is trapped
to end here

- Z. Rose

Glory of the Snow:

standing like a frozen model
fair skin, but bright smile
for all to see
no one has seen her move

always there in the spotlight
always there leading
up from the ashes of snow
the dormant feelings of depression

She dreams of making it from the ground up
She dreams of sprouting through the snow

frozen with glory in our minds

- Z. Rose

Dear frozen flor-a,

I see the ice biting into your wilting bloom. Your color stolen by the son of the Sun, yet you are bright. Staying grounded through the snow in these times is hard. Hope of a new Spring is hard to see. Through your frozen smile I see this next Spring will have new opportunities. Those that think about your next move, also don't know how to lead themselves.

You take the spotlight from other flor-as. Rising up from the ashes of snow was a tragic winter, but when you came back in Spring I saw your true strength. It didn't matter about what anyone else thought or did, because you did it. You taught us all to keep dreams alive. Thank you for coming back this Spring. You will always be a glorified memory. Saved frozen in the snow, and in our minds.

~ from one flor-a to another

Impatient:

waiting around for you to buzz home
i've been awake all day, lonesome
i like to be watched
as i work outside

as i dance in the mid-day breeze
as i shower to smell nice for you
as i get my hair and make-up done by the Sun
i've been waiting to be picked
out of all the other flowers to be

i want to be there
for you
i can't wait to see you, again

- Z. Rose

Latana, My Light:

you light my world
the way you light my world gives me energy
the energy to light up for others
leading them on a magical path

send lightning messages
to give others energy
to motivate others
lead them on a successful path

growing beauty, with age
don't lock yourself in a cage

we want to grow
so let the energy flow

- Z. Rose

Those that Lead are Worthy:

asking for directions
i don't know how to lead
listen to the wind
listen to the birds
listen to the clouds
listen to the ground
not every weed is a dictator
following the flowers is helpful to grow a garden
together we will decide where to go
but for now let's enjoy where we are

- Z. Rose

Maiden in Pink:

fitting in the best boots
bright from the petals to the roots
fitting in the ground firm and sound
brought to greet each other's wounds
fitting to be the forbidden love in all the lands
working around the clock
fitting in appointments for all to block
complex with a secret love language only a few speak

- Z. Rose

41

Pin the Cushions:

you have stabbed me multiple times
for the problems i cannot fix
for the ideas you do not like
for the love you hated others had for me
poking me when i do something wrong
shaming me when i forget something
lying to me because i'm little
yet i'm experienced

are you happy now?

i give myself to you
pale and unrooted

plant me, in the wetlands
so i can clean my wounds

    - Z. Rose

Shooting Star:

i see you've come down from Heaven
shot out of the sky
wounded but planting your roots
shining like a star with foreign beauty
may i wish upon such rarity
in return, i promise to help you grow

   - Z. Rose

Facing Facts:

from the Garden of Eden
forbidden and picked
fought to restore health and beauty

- Z. Rose

Spring's Snowflake:

dressing up to go outside
knowing it's the first time the sun will give a kiss
months without my moonlight walks
months without my hot showers
months without my Love picking me
months without my dance in the dirt
knowing this is the first of Spring
out dressing the snowflakes

- Z. Rose

Dear Archangel,

Please watch over me as i turn my back
on love
on people
on nature
on life

Please watch over me as i enter a habitat
of love
of people
of nature
of life

Please watch over me as i give up
on love
on people
on nature
on life

Please watch over me as i diverge
from love
from people
from nature
from life

Please my Archangel,
watch over me as i turn Yellow.

- Z. Rose

Dear archangel,

Thank you for saving my life. I saw no beauty or reason to stop and smell the roses. You have taught me, the little gestures in life are remembered more than anything else. I broke a lot of hearts in my previous years, and you showed me how to mend mine.

Mending my heart helped pave the path to the people I love. I found my nature was not following me, rather I needed to follow my own nature. This put me back on my path of life. Here I found many more flor-as. Each unequally beautiful. Each of us trying to grow through different dirt. Yet the seasons are the same.

Each day I recite my prayers and my affirmation I have come up with a plan. If we bring all the flor-as together, we won't feel lonely when struggling. I hope the others find strength and prosperity as I have in you.

Please archangel—watch over us all.

~ flor-a

Lose Yourself:

Lose yourself in my color
Lose yourself in my love
Lose yourself in my pistil
Lose yourself in my dirt

- Z. Rose

Oh Zinnia, My Love:

the way you fill a crowd
       with your life
the way you fill a room
       with your smile
the way you fill a town
       with your humor
the way you fill the dirt
       with your roots
the way you fill the sea
       with your tears
the way you fill the sky
       with your dreams
the way you fill my heart
       with your love
the way i overfill your style
       with my love

          - Z. Rose

Crying for Rain:

crying he will come back for you
strike you with his lightning
finding pleasure in your pain
but Rain doesn't understand
growing between the cracks and ask for help
dodging every foot that dangers your seed
choking on tears that may satisfy his taste
but Rain doesn't understand the struggle
to grow when he comes back
for you

        - Z. Rose

Gerbera Daisies:

i have a type
loud and proud
i am a type
loud and proud

like the rest
i must confess
i am who i am
love who i love

i fit in
into the ground
next to the others
just as profound

speaking up
rising up
blooming together
sprouting out
loud and proud

i may lose
but just a few petals in the breeze
i may lose
but never give up and freeze
i may lose
but never the sight of others' needs

   - Z. Rose

When the Lilly Lied:

sitting in the flower-bed
watching the sun set
asking myself what tomorrow brings
opening my mouth to sing
the cat jumped by and cut my tongue

they say it's an old saying
lie like a rug
but i saw Lilly on the rug
dancing across the print
changing colors as i blinked

drawing a bath
with some dry grass
no one seen in days
dried up
i had to lie
and take a sip

finding the Lilly wasn't where i laid
drowned in a pond
stung by a bee
pushed around by the wind
to be everywhere, but not really her

laying low
closing up
shutting down

goodnight, Lilly

was that your lie?

　　- Z. Rose

Lilly,

Please don't lie. There isn't a reason. Most of the time the fear that causes a lie is made up in that pistil. If you take advice from the pistil understand it's very reason is temptation to lie. Leaving no inspiration around. Without inspiration, your bloom will die.

Please save yourself. Lead with heart, and don't lie. We love you for your perspective. It is different. Without a shout or shoot, I want to hear you. I want you to be yourself around me.

Has it been so long you've changed completely. Get up from that rug Lilly. You can rest in the flower-bed with me. We can talk it out. Please don't shut down.

~ Mother Nature

Vibrant, Violent Colors:

to all the colors planted in the ground:

i'm j e a l o u s
not only are you living
but you're everywhere

vibrantly taking over the walls
violently covering bodies

vibrantly bringing people together
violently distancing cultures

vibrantly showing individual uniqueness
violently troubling mental states

vibrantly luminating the sky for all to see
violently shutting down communication

growing in popularity
becoming everyone's favorite

clout so thick there's no sun
i'm glad you're grounded somewhere

    - Z. Rose

to be so sweet
polite when others beat
curtsy when i see another
stand when i see my brother

ruffling over the edges
blooming to be fancy
i know i'm finer than wine
over spilling the ledges

elegant to the eye
beauty to buy
bubbling to my feet
to be so sweet

   - Z. Rose

Bulbs:

dropping down like a disco ball
he is seen
draw the attention from Spring
dance 'til dawn
then 'til dusk
be the elegant lady you are
crushed between a rock and dirt
making the best of the situation
celebrating the attitude bulb's carry

- Z. Rose

Balloons are Flowers too:

open and gasping for air
hoping i take flight
holding onto the stem as a string
cradled in the petals of a flower
safe and sound from floating too high
playfully picked up in a gust of wind
easily swaying back and forth as i've taken flight
a breath of fresh air

- Z. Rose

Combine to be Kind:

the cast you film are one of a kind
ones' with talent
highest ratings
longest showing

the show is one of a kind
planting itself in a new habitat
teaching others of the plot
planted firmly in this pot

the best and brightest of its kind
this production is vivid
hyping up the innocent
and the trouble intertwines

   - Z. Rose

Change Gossip:

tickling the ears of the Devil
speaking his name in vain
dishing out gossip like it's a game

change

up and down the stalk
on a walk
taking thorns, instead of giving them

change

rooting in the problem
never realizing to stem
grow above and bloom to be the emblem

change

the Season's mind
growing a name
that's no game

   - Z. Rose

Dear little flor-as,

Gossip travels fast with the wind. Taking the news of who stroked your stalk to the next walkway. Each flower entering the garden will grow an emblem to be known by. Actions speak louder than words, because the words the wind blows might not be true. It's like a game.

So we must change the game and Season's mind.

~ from a mangled flor-a mind still trying to change

i lied awake with the moon
its light shined so bright, it brought hours of ponder
am i in the right
to know that the garden that stands outside has wilted
in hopes that my spirit is lifted

- B. Monét

held from me, hidden
you confide in me
the key to my heart
this pistil locks up
all your secrets, shut

- B. Monét

a glass punctured by a thorn
shattered into a million and one pieces
one cuts my flesh
the breeze hits, it feels so fresh
swish
the bottom of the bottle i see
double vision begins to cloud me
stumbling through time
faces begin to blur
my words begin to slur
my sanity questions reality
unknown, my heart is made of glass
shattered into a million pieces
punctured by a thorn

        - B. Monét

Dear Beauty,

you are a blank canvas
in the meadow waiting for a fairy to use her magic
finding Beauty whispering behind the trees
seeking Beauty in the buds
bursting through the dirt
floating towards the light
engulfing Beauty with love

- Mother Nature

- Z. Rose

Aster:

lying flat on my back
pushed against the dirt
soiled and turned over
coving myself with leaves
finding scrapes on my face
sprouting branches from my back
not knowing what i turned into
but knowing one day i will bloom
again

   - Z. Rose

Blind to Me:

feeling alone
no one is home
knocking down doors
no one is home
screaming for help
no one is home
lying alone
no one is home

where did they all go?
the help
the support
the love
the hope
must be blooming, into oblivion

   - Z. Rose

Calla:

leading the classes
following the crown
sitting at the highest peak
not to jump, but to seek
all dignity found at her roots
crowning Calla with Glory
in the Garden of Beauty
leading 'til the end of time

    - Z. Rose

Dear Chloris,

i planted myself in the Elysian Fields
rooted in, i fight for my pot
transplanted overnight
left me to drip poison like sap
rooting them, like they me
forced for pleasure
never fought for a breath

i felt the way you broke
sacrificed in my garden
in a sense i'm over picked
my Elysium in two

- Love

- Z. Rose

Clever Clover:

ever so clever
i saw a clover
at the end of a rainbow
i saw a clover

daring to be picked
i run over
to the clover
picking the stem
of the clover
moving closer
to the clover

i make a wish
to the clover
l u c k y
to be the clover
overhearing
the ever so clever
clover speaks

- Z. Rose

grow with strength, young one
find patience in time
bloom when you are ready

sprout to meet the Bee's kiss
know he will leave, yet try to come back
keep him safe in your petals, you are strong

patient in winter
to spring into love
bloom when you are ready

- Z. Rose

Gardenia:

cultivating year after year
celebrating summer after summer
creating spring after spring
continue the garden
even after you think you are done

   - Z. Rose

Hazel by Witch:

    the hazel eye
   needs protection
   petals surround
pointing to the hole in the center

    share some dirt
    yank some weeds
    blow the blooms
    drain the seeds

looking for someone
   to protect me
     to see me
the hazel in my eye

        - Z. Rose

Core Blossom:

the apple of my eye
cut to the core
saving the seeds
to have another start
b l o o m
the apple of my eye

- Z. Rose

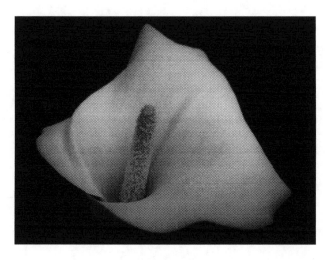

Holly:

kissing under the bridge
so no one can see
hiding a seed of feelings
secretly growing
celebrating a wedding above the bridge

- Z. Rose

Jasmine's Peace:

peaceful waters
like to rustle at night
running down her stem
dripping from her petals
dowsing below her roots
fending for her seed
silent waters keep secrets
keeping her mind at peace

- Z. Rose

The Common are Mellow:

picked for pleasure
i'm known by the people
i must stay low
stay grounded
stay

for the mellow group sees
an altered state
effected through time
through movement
through

for the obstacles teach
a shared story
of a relatable flower picked apart
picked by me
picked

    - Z. Rose

In a Bind:

i haven't heard from you in a while
how have you been?
i saw you've been posting a lot
how's the new life?
i see things have changed
how can i get a hold of you?
i found myself in a bind
how did you dig yourself out?
i remember us back in high school
how did you change?
i always seem to get myself in a bind
how about some advice?
i want to grow

how did you blossom so fast?
i take my time
how did you see the light from beneath?
i sprouted around
how did you find someone to help you in a bind?

i saw you got a transplant
how did that go?
i know you root quickly
how did you recover?
i am asking
how can i get help out of my bind?

- Z. Rose

Blue Gem:

love by the sea, where she is lost
unable to see her tears
blending right in
next to the sand
the grains hard to catch
slipping through
unable to root
floating out to sea
wishing for the waves
to take her away, from this exotic love

- Z. Rose

Light the Night:

i'm a natural piece of art
Vibrant
Bold
Unique
Bright
energy flows through me

as the Sun paints my petals
with rain made of polish
i dance in the wind
dying to dry
ready to grow in Spring's gallery

   - Z. Rose

Bermuda Buttercup:

rich with mystery
captivating the Captain
sailing by shore
lying on land
drowning to death

sneaky smooth
stealing stuff
bringing back
my memories
Bermuda Buttercup

seeds to start
sprouting for sun
simple in Spring
sailing to Satin
a mystery, not worth the treasure

- Z. Rose

The Buzz of You:

sweet like honey
vibrant as a chameleon
attractive to all
yet
sour like a lemon
dull as a sloth
unattractive to all

you belong

between my lips
stealing the spotlight
loving yourself
because the bees do

your very stigma
enhances
your very being
and your beliefs
yet
your very being
enhances
your stigma
and your beliefs

you belong

trust yourself
you're rooted
connect with others
accept yourself

because the Queen does
because Mother Nature does
because the Universe does
because you will

- B. Monét & Z. Rose

Lead to See:

pure petals
twist and turn
not so nice

but from afar you can see
her gleam
sending signals
through her style
looks tend to deceive
beauty as pure

yet we're all rooted in dirt
yet we all come from dirt
better-yet, the same dirt

- Z. Rose

Iris is Gone:

growing up unable to side
one perspective for another

similar stories
with fancy names in the stories
dressing Cruelty in the finest gown
building up, unable to subside
e d e m a
it's over
Iris passed

   - Z. Rose

Frilly Filler Flower:

the fluff
says no stuff
in the middle

planting dreams
playing the fiddle
peeking through
pardon me

leaves tickle too
fill the space
with your face

   - Z. Rose

Anyone with Me:

we watch in awe
as Spring brings Sun
the smile of life
together now
adding anew
seeds grow apart
upright in awe

- Z. Rose

Living Lotus:

celebrating the way you dance
rooted in the ground
life to another life

mind, body, spirit

enlightenment seen in your eyes
connected to nature
life to another life

mind, body, spirit

thankful for another twirl
spreading your seed
to bring life

mind, body, spirit

celebrating the way you are

- Z. Rose

arrange the arrangement
nice and neat
dreamt of a day
i would have purpose
to protest a walk
i would make it an event
the day i dreamt
nice and neat
with my arrangements

a gold ring around the middle
promising to tend my garden
you are my Marigold
until the end of my days

- Z. Rose

Pen it Up for Work:

working hard
to fit in
like a black sheep
in a white herd
wiping clean
to fit in
like a dictator
making a Master Race
being one of a kind
like a stem
growing a vibrant pistil

- Z. Rose

Mary Rose:

dead to most
lost out at sea

sea, she gains power
as she eats those thrown to her
feeding on the morning dew
beautiful violet shadows under her eye
forcing out the evil
keeping the young to survive
don't drown, Dear
for your roots are rotted

left to die
out at sea

    - Z. Rose

Primrose:

sewn together at the edges
leaving a seam to rip
Beauty lays the petals wisely
keeping everything together
but losing one petal at a time
the first is last
and the last is first
for you have it all, Primrose

    - Z. Rose

Willow:

it looks like you've gotten whipped
what did you do?

why didn't you stop him?

consciousness takes over
logic overriding all weakness
growing through rock
patient with the seasons
splitting ready for transfer
grounded for peace
retreat to the widow

- Z. Rose

Bud:

hey there, Bud
just started to sprout the news
we all lose
even if you are a stud

- Z. Rose

Replant This Madness:

let's not be anticlimactic
you motivate me
to work hard
to communicate
to believe
to love

you humble me
to help others
to help myself
to love others
to love myself

you ground me
to sprout
to bloom
to blossom
to spring
let's replant next season

- Z. Rose

Hypnotized:

looped into a plan

tightly wound
in my gown
how did i fall in this hole
who knew i'd grow
sprouting potential
branching out
cultivating ideas
following the flower

with the masterminds

- Z. Rose

Flower China:

sound the bells
dust off the Fine China resting on the shelves
water the vines drooping from the walls
set up the chairs in the hall
leading me to the ball
gathering those from afar

sound the bells
i am the star
sent from Hell
sound the bells

roll out the long
Gold
Carpet
sound the bells
let the world know that i have b l o o m e d
through Hell and back

— B. Monét

time bends you in
fear kicks in
my adrenaline blinds
chills run down the stem of my spine
anticipating whether an insult will stick me a splinter
sour my expression
and rage will pour out my mouth

holding grudges not worth my time
seasons come and go
don't be a foe
time is a construct, don't you know

– B. Monét

Dear foe,

Time is constantly moving, changing our daily perspective
Seasons do come and go— always looking forward
Yet we linger in the past, dwell on our past
We fall into a rabbit hole of emotions,
going through the motions,
not knowing what I am missing right in front on me
A splinter stabbing me into reality

It's time to go,
Seasons

why is it that i see you as a
w i l d f l o w e r
yet you see yourself as a
w e e d

- B. Monét

roses Red
violets Blue
who knew these riots would bring joy to you
the Sun's flower Yellow
the Moon's garden White
falling like bullets, these tears run dry
the dew coats the trenches
dividing the United in half

broken love in two

- B. Monét

i am
a galaxy full of time
a garden full of life
a sea full of secrets
a desert full of wonders

- B. Monét

save me
i'm lost
this garden is fully grown
once sane, insane tone
thoughts are a blur
the mind goes *mur*
save me

- B. Monét

creeping up silently from afar
the howling winds become calm
the rustling of the trees stand still
the crying in the distance drown out

my bed of peonies once open, shut
the sun sets, giving up
close to quarrel
petals tussle and rustle

like a storm known for chaos
the urge to fulfill your needs silences

   - B. Monét

Dear P.,

I see you on your toes-uprooted.

I predict your next move
Slowly creeping through life
I influence you to move
To move forward yet stuck in the past
The past seems to fly by fast
Only to lead up to this moment
A moment in time where you

Sink your toes and be deeply-rooted.

A life full of chaos i bring to you.

~ Storm

Love is a Sight, Worth a Fight:

my eyes sore for a sight
the last bloom is a sight

spring at me
coat me in May
set me free
before i lay

caressed by kisses
imprinted a stain
forced by blame
bruised lips have pain

the will to be
the golden ray
allowed me to see
convinced me to stay

if love is worth a fight
i'll give it my best fight

    - B. Monét

```
        tugged,  taunted,  tamed
        a  life  full  of  torture
              broken  loose
                    one
                    by
                    one
              my  petals
                                        f
                          a
                    l
              l

              f  l  o  a  t~ing,

catching              the              current

                    GASP
              full  of  potential
        ideas  made  to  be  set  f  r  e  e

                    -  B.  Monét
```

My Darlin' Deserves a Daisy:

Dandy Darlin'
Dandy Daisy

Dangling Down
Dwelling Develops
Drowning i frown

Dangerous Droughts
Deep Down
Digging Dirt

Dainty Daisy
Dark Darlin'

- B. Monét

a - c a t a s   t   r   o   p   h   e
these years have been, despite life
in light of it all

you feel
f r e e
to breathe

these lungs were failing
even the trees work harder
growing for years now

we suffer
p a i n
and consequences

these roots are drowning
not sprouting petals in Spring
please believe in me

i am
b e a u t y
at its worst
and finest
m o m e n t s
in time

    - B. Monét

i feel the tension in the air
come closer if you dare
i hear the whispers LOUD and c l e a r
with no fear
judging away
lashing the words you say
depicting every scar
built from afar
my delicate petals tussle to the ground
laying there i found
gossip was never fair
yet i gave it my best share
words puncture pain
fire burns me insane
a bulb torched into the ground

    - B. Monét

magic is surreal
your growth is proof of the deal
life's bloom is so real

- B. Monét

this breeze caresses my petals, easing my pain
reminiscing my growth, the rush it blows
this breeze caresses my stem, supportively

p r o u d

on the edge of this hilltop, i rest overlooking the sunset
the horizon full of water for miles, i stand waiting
on the edge of this world, i wonder beyond the galaxy
the horizon full of life, i visualize the vast possibilities

i could be

- B. Monét

it's a habit, a bad habit
it's more consistent to till me down
rather than lift me up

recalling a time, speaking of a conundrum
i bloom awake at night
i hear howling in the wind
the breeze recalls about a time
a time i could not control

drowning in my mistakes
i sprout out of comfort
a life to preserve

not to drown, rather, sprout out
a new habit
to plant
to grow
to sprout

beauty is destruction
from a bad habit
is my habit

- B. Monét

To my bad habits:

Thank you for highlighting my imperfections. A change worth fighting for, I observe and accept who I am. I am not perfect. A life full of lessons, I thrive on my own mistakes. Beauty is my destruction—a life pure with purpose. I am here to grow and learn. To live a life without regret, is to live a life without fear.

pick the wind
picture a bloom

beaming in the sun
that one is for you
see it in your dreams

don't pick
or the wind will tear you
a tornado uprooting your bed

protected by an omnipotent
blossomed for you
in your dreams

pick the wind
picture a bloom

   - Z. Rose

6 Feet Under:

far below eyesight
no hope, only darkness
stubborn life will live
thrusting up through the soil
breaking the expectation
germinating twice as fast
flourishing beyond comfort
stubborn with life
see me now, above the soil
far above eyesight

   - Z. Rose

picked for glory
we rise in glory
Spring is here
the flowers are here
picked for glory
people pick

for love
for beauty
for greed
for more

- Z. Rose

                  producing pollen
    not knowing, the wind sends my sent your way

              what is thought of me

          propping my petals higher
           busting my stem higher
          drawing my pistil higher
         sprouting my stigma higher

   dancing in the wind, anything to catch your eye
        not knowing what message i sent your way

                    - Z. Rose

competing in my garden

First to sprout
First to produce
First to pick
First to eat

living in my garden

- Z. Rose

Dear Sunshine,

i miss the days you kiss my tips, resting my pistol on your chest. dancing in the cold wind, seeing you smile next to me in bed. i miss waking to your light, feeding my inner demons to Hell. uplifting me to save our love story - i know we have our good and bad days. but i need you. i need your tears to heal my roots. i need your anger to melt my frost. so we fight to be closer. i need the rays to know you are mine.

Love,

- Your Bloom

- B. Monét

Dear Bloom,

I sense your aura in the air, sadly my tears have run dry. My energy has gone numb. I miss being the first to wake you in the morning; I would liberate you from your night terror every morning. Unfortunately the days are long and the nights are long. I know you need me, i sure need you, but time is not on our side. Time passes by so easily. I forgot when was the last time we met. Promise not to forget me, I swear I will not forget you; until we meet again.

Yours truly,
Sunshine

crushing dried petals
using them to heal my wounds
delicately healed

- Z. Rose

loving from afar
thrown a rose
catching the thorn on my hand
wounded, love will bloom

- Z. Rose

folding in on my dreams
putting my pistil in a cage

puffing my pollen

the stigma
the style
the stamen
the anther

through a tube
out my ovary
back down my stem
shriveling my roots

let me out

unfolding what i once knew
to obtain what i never knew

- Z. Rose

Oriental Eyes:

because i see you
in my sweet dreams
dancing alone
learning patience
growing upward

because i want to experience
my dreams with you
dancing together
learning together
growing together

because Love sees
us fulfill our dreams
us take steps forward
us rooting down
us growing up

   - Z. Rose

bug eyed, at eye level
kneeled, to the queen

a ring of petals

spring, by her nose
in hopes, to hear the buzz

will you marry me?

- Z. Rose

flower children
bloom with the birds
grow with the grasshoppers
skip with the seeds
laugh with the lightning bugs
race with the rabbits
jump with the June bugs
sway with the stems
we are the children of the flowers

- Z. Rose

Water-Colors:

colors taint my veins
blabbering the blues
binging the greens
bruising the purples
blocking the browns
bleeding through to my petals

- Z. Rose

Shapes Bloom:

blooming into a shape

use your imagination
draw a stem
up to the leaf
start with the bud
don't stop at one bloom

onto the next
imagine the evolution
a new life takes shape, side by side
we have a guide
that's how the blooms thrive

blooming into a shape

   - B. Monét and Z. Rose

Beauty:

like a blanket of fog

covering my roots
crowding my stem
cursing my buds
crushing my blooms

i find beauty in the haze

- Z. Rose

planted to question

bombing the blooms

assassinating the aliens
terminating the disease
stretching my roots
collecting my seeds

uprooted for me to answer

ending the pain

- Z. Rose

sensing my sadness
the sky shades grey
the winds howl
the clouds clap

the stars raise the bet
a deadline to be met
shoots like a threat

netting up my hair
tugging on my loose stems
netting up my ideas
tugging on my loose petals

shedding a tear
raging the storm
here to bring me home

i lay low, in shelter
from all this chaos
about to blow over

- B. Monét

resilient are my ruffles
bloom open for all to see
time truly does show change

i have to unfold
b o l d
i'm told
i hold

like a siren, luring you in
you fear the truth
a dangerous sin
beauty is in the eye
a resilient lie

- B. Monét

look how much i've grown, i conquer my daily fear
dancing in the wind, thriving audaciously
assuming i'm crazy, but the seedlings say not

the horizon brings optimism, yet I cry with deficit and guilt
your floral scent blew, radiantly free
envy burns my roots, unable to bloom through the glass ground

- B. Monét

i wilt in distrust
a vision pictured clear through a crystal ball
a series of unfortunate events
a rumble in the sky, loud aching

you wallow in distrust

your love for me was predicted
your time for me was conflicted
your bees buzzed the news
you have always been bad news

i wallow in distrust

- B. Monét

torn in half, aching
my heart cannot take much more
i wilt in distrust

i wilt in distrust
a vision pictured clear through a crystal ball
a series of unfortunate events
a rumble in the sky, loud aching

you wallow in distrust

your love for me was predicted
your time for me was conflicted
your bees buzzed the news
you have always been bad news

i wallow in distrust

— B. Monét

To Distrust,

It's an instinct- gut feeling
To question your every move
To wonder if you'll come back

Trust was never my specialty

Deception spills off those lips
News seems to travel far
Only i'd hope it wouldn't be true

Trust was never my specialty

Love,
Hope

Falling for My Trap:

the similarity between my love and your bargain
is the advantage i deal
this petal

the difference between my lust and your bargain
is the disadvantage i'm dealt
dirt

the difference between my lust and your bargain
is the advantage i'm dealt
in seasons

the similarity between my love and your bargain
is the disadvantage i deal
at this table

    - Lip Biting Card Dealer
    - a.k.a: B. Monét

hear me whistling through the wind, blowing my horn
a call for celebration, showing that i have grown
a two-step, care to join
i whisk through the wind
once familiar to the tune, now foreign to my roots

   - B. Monét

Desert Flower:

batting the eye, not sure i'd survive
i thrive the most, unimaginable to the eye

- B. Monét

given
purpose
to bloom
to live
an adventurous life

given
one time
to bloom
to live
dying an adventurous life

- B. Monét

bare, bold, bright
blooms bargain, bonds build

shy, sound, set
she sways solo, stubbornness shadows

- B. Monét

Remembrance:

what is it you need
advice
support
supply
loyalty
unknowingly good for one thing
your garden
hoping to be seen

what is it you need
pleasure
attention
fantasy
thrill
unknowingly good for one thing
your bouquet
my seed laying here

i'm out of what you need
tears
envy
love
comfort
unknowingly good for one thing
your flower
torn apart by you

- B. Monét & Z. Rose

it's always been you, Sweet Pea
i knew it the moment i saw you
my mouth began to water
drawn to you, by my nose

you smell like Spring
blowing through the breeze
how we instantly lock eyes
how you smile, batting your eyes
i see your bells ring
attracting all the bees
your scent so, so-so sweet, Pea

- B. Monét

Dear Sweet Pea,

I want to say a lot of thing, but only so much will fit on this page and in an envelope for you. I would do anything for us to be together again. You sing in Spring, I miss your voice. Even how your laugh carries like bells. I see your eyes light up like stars in the sky. Batting away the ideas running through my head, we lock eyes. It's as if in that moment you know what I'm thinking. Attracted to your lips as bees are to a flor-a. Remembering your sent as it blows through the breeze. I forget everything I want to say.

~ secret admirer

gather around let's play a game
under, over
up, down
grab the lie by the root
tips tricks
going over
going down
it's only but a game

like a merry go round
around we go
we grow up
like a flower
lose our petals
and our minds
going around
this merry go round

- B. Monét

Merry-A-Gold:

i marry Gold for
    the diamonds
      the rubies
        the fur
      the money

i married Gold for
  the independence
 the opportunities
   the adventures
   the impossible

 Gold isn't merry
 i'm dead by Gold
   in Dirt's safe

      - Z. Rose

the end of the rainbow is a sight
there my petals shine bright
painted in gold
polished i'm sold
lured in with flirtation
a beauty filled with temptation

        - B. Monét

                    there my petals shine bright
                            painted in gold
                a beauty filled with temptation
                            polished i'm sold
                        lured in with flirtation
            the end of the rainbow is a sight

                            - B. Monét

a flower so delicate
even the bees must stay away
keeping each other passionate
a flower kept at bay

nervous to touch
thorns bring fear
the pain is not much
but a flower sheds a tear

a flower so fragile
even the bees must suppress
their lust so bashful
a flower is kept in distress

- B. Monét

a petal must flirt
dazzle the damsel with love
temptation will drip

   - Z. Rose

flirtation you drip
a hummingbird draws nectar
temptation i drip

   - B. Monét

flirtatious humming
tempting the root of my mouth
a bird draws nectar

- B. Monét & Z. Rose

Anecdote:

laying away
in the daybed
laying away
parallel from my love
laying away
dead in my bed

far away

growing desperate
losing my roots
pulling my leaves
tearing my stem

my anecdote
lucid, like lean
sweet, like honey
pleasant, for all to see

   - Z. Rose

Lie in Leaves:

so genuine and wise
what a pleasant surprise
so brilliant and courageous
your roots subtly draw me in
so long and strong
lying to be fairer
so sweet and rare

- Z. Rose

Secrets of the Sun:

the Sun keeps secrets of controversy
on your lips, is everything i want to hear
you spring on me, all the news
now running to the Rain
spilling all your tears
lashing-out in lust

but your lips, end the season

overgrown, from your promises
overwhelmed, by your stories
devastated, over the memories
absorbed, are the secrets told
to another bloom, in dormant
the Sun kept controversy in the garden

- Z. Rose

i visit, tickling your nose

masked by the scent of rain
smell me for Spring's sneeze
inhale pollen to remain

masked by the scent after a fire
smell me in Summer's breeze
exhale the smoke of the bushfire

masked by the scent of spice
smell me in Fall's feast
inhale the sweet sugar allspice

masked by a sent, i lie
smell me in Winter's freeze
exhale the wind blowing dry

i visit, tickling your nose
bitter, sweet, sour
all year round

- B. Monét

Lost Petal:

little lost
around the corner, my stem waits
for me to grow up

i haven't explored yet
around the corner, is another corner
my stem waits

but i will not go back
empowering my stigma to be strong
to bloom multiple times a year

through it all
i will find my way
having learned from my stem

- Z. Rose

Take My Breath:

the moment you stand
taller than before
measure life and breath
to bloom
my breath away

   - Z. Rose

Dying, Dead Flower:

you dazzle in the dark
brush paint to illuminate the room

oh so faint

at the base of my bud
held in
spilling my seeds
held in
from the mark left

let her paint

to illuminate the room
to dazzle you, in the dark

- Z. Rose

like layers
a peony, sheds
memories
pain
joy
flirtation

like she lays
full of memories
remembering the pain
full of joy
recalling flirtation

full of memories
craving flirtation
full of joy
recalling the pain

- B. Monét

lost, the will to grow
my roots creep, in silence
unable to grow

my upbringing was silenced
let it be known i was unattended
i won't ever be mended

i've lost it
my roots sprout, in freedom
mending my bloom

   - B. Monét

Fossil Seed:

i dance in the wind, i giggle as i glide
i arch as i spin, my seed stretches up and out
so mellow and slow, each corner i touch
an imprint i leave on a leaf, for others to follow

throw me in the wind, i'll giggle as i glide
another chance to stretch, to live free of sin
spiraling out of control, imprint every touch
another to follow, i leave

a memory in the wind, my giggle lies in the trees
staying still in time, my seed lays flat and dries
so mellow and slow, each corner i touch
left an imprint on leaves, for others to follow

- B. Monét & Z. Rose

a shadow
not mine
lingers beside me
watching every move i make

enforcing a mistake

move with the wind,
are you trying to uproot?
ration the water,
are you an animal?

lingering over
i wilt my blooms down
not trying to be seen
but i always seem to be found

to enforce forgiveness on all the mistakes

       - B. Monét

```
from growth, we root
from floret, we rise
from wonder, we bloom
from wisdom, we love

    - Z. Rose
```

roses are red
violets are blue
you see me
but i see through you

i know where your roots have been

soil spills secrets and strong sentiment
sorry your reputation will be forgotten

forget me not, in the wind
forget me not, in the song of bird
forget me not, in the water that drips
forget me not, in the fertile soil

i know where your roots are

red are the valley's that run dry
blue are the ocean's violet eyes
you see me
but i see through you

- B. Monét & Z. Rose

reminiscing on our youth
when the world was ours
forever

an illusion we planted

to root deep, before the mountains have collapsed
to sprout full of life, before the rivers have run dry
to b l o o m bright, before the gardenias have wilted

awaken within seconds, it perishes
once lost with you, now lost without you
we've come to the end of the book

- B. Monét

index:

Printed in the United States
by Baker & Taylor Publisher Services